Praise for *Waiting for Morning*

"The wrecked and wretched of the world . . . speak holy words," and Bob Rees has the sagacity to hear them and render their holiness in poetry. What Eugene England did for the personal essay, Rees does for poetry—dedicating its shapes to the sacred work of witness, Mormon conscience, and presence. These pages remember the mother he lost, the wife he survived, and the war-afflicted and imprisoned in places near and far away. They are suffused with the tireless industry, expansive vision and pragmatic elegance of the Mormon people. I am grateful.—Joanna Brooks, co-editor, *Mormon Feminism: Essential Writings*, and author, *The Book of Mormon Girl*

In his poetry Bob Rees plumbs the depths of his responsive soul while painting the landscapes of his courageous life. He has mastered the vocabulary of poesy in an evocative way. Whoever reads his work will enter a life well lived and generously shared.—Mary Bradford, poet, author of the collection *Purple*

Robert Rees's *Waiting for Morning* pays homage to all human experience—life to death—reading mysteries in "the calligraphy of seagrass," finding solace in the "systolic and diastolic pulse of creation," expressing infinities in the "the runed and ruined language of the world." His poems reflect a keen observer's open heart, seeing pain in beauty and beauty in pain, and finding, in each, minute moments of truth. The poignancy of "A Mirror for Josephine Miles" elicits tears of gratitude for human courage and brilliance, while "Universe" sees in a week-old grandson a universe "that will expand infinitely."—Michael R. Collings World Horror Con Grand Master and Multiple Bram Stoker Award finalist for poetry

There is much to admire in Bob Rees's collection, especially (for me) the first two sections, "Experience" and "Abandoned." And Clifton Jolley's introduction is indispensable for understanding Bob's poetry in the context of American literary history and criticism. The overall value of *Waiting for Morning* comes from Bob's skill as a poet: his deep and broad experience as a humanitarian and educator; his overcoming of a traumatic childhood; and, finally, and most importantly, his lifelong determination to place the Restored Gospel of Jesus Christ first in his heart and mind, no matter what. *Waiting for Morning* is a worthy addition to the many intellectual and artistic services Robert A. Rees has provided to thoughtful Mormons throughout his life.—R. A. Christmas, author of seven books of poetry

Stirred to fullness and passion by life's abundance, Whitman sang, "I will go to the bank by the wood and become undisguised and naked, / I am mad for it to be in contact with me." His "it," of course, is the world, beating and breathing all around him. Bob Rees exhibits a similar madness in *Waiting for Morning*: a madness to be in contact with life in its many manifestations, to hold it close, and to be nourished by that closeness. Stripped of pretension, Rees's poems lay bare a mind exposed to his physical, cultural, and spiritual environments. They show him in celebration and grief, deep longing and joy, but always basking in words.—Tyler Chadwick is the editor of *Fire in the Pasture: 21st Century Mormon Poets,* and co-editor of the forthcoming *Dove Song: Heavenly Mother in Mormon Poetry*

Waiting for Morning

Poems by
ROBERT A. REES

Cover designed by Thayne Whiting
Design and layout by Brent Corcoran
ISBN 978-0-9993472-0-1

Printed in the U.S.A.

Zarahemla Books
869 East 2680 North
Provo, UT 84604 U.S.A.
info@zarahemlabooks.com
ZarahemlaBooks.com

For Jenny, Bobby, Anna & Maddy
my first and best poems

Every poet is aware of his or her indebtedness to other poets and to any muse who inspires. The list of poets living and dead to whom I am indebted are too numerous to mention, but I will mention several poet-friends who have been particularly influential, by encouragement, example or specific suggestions for shaping some of the poems in this volume: Mary Bradford, friend and fellow poet for half a century; Robert Christmas, whose "Mormon" poems have inspired me to try and write about my own religious culture; and Clifton Jolley, whose careful ear, observant eye and brutal honesty helped make some of these poems better than I could have made them myself.

Table Of Contents

NATURE

RELIGIOUS

FOREWORD

The Prismed Pastoral:
Peace and the Poetry of Robert Rees

Clifton H. Jolley

"Peace I leave with you
My peace I give unto you.
Not as the world giveth...."

Robert Rees is a scholar of American Romanticism, but he is not a romantic in the literary sense of the word. He does not participate in a romantic regret for a fallen world in which entropy drives only decay. Of such a world Shelley mourned that "Nought may endure but Mutability" and Wordsworth lamented "... the unimaginable touch of Time." Even Robert Frost argued that "nothing gold can stay." But Bob Rees exults:

> This world's turning:
> from bright orange to burnt umber,
> from terra sienna to cinnamon,
> from astringent to sweet,
> from branch to ground,
> root to flower to fruit.

And again ...

> and at once all the trees of the field
> clap their hands and rejoice,
> sending their roots along the stream,
> their foliage ever green
> against the dying year.

He does not accept that gold turns to dross, that youth is defeated by age, that virtue is overwhelmed by vice, or that what we expect is defeated by what we have no way of anticipating. Rather, in Bob's world, "All his perils and travails will give him experience and be for his good." However dark the moment, Bob Rees is looking towards a light that many times is invisible to the rest of us, and that is all the more reason to value the experience and enlightenment of these poems.

Shelley died too young to test or regret his premise. Wordsworth stopped writing memorable poems well before he died in his eightieth year. And mischievous Robert Frost is reported to have hid in the woods, tormenting his children by pretending to have been eaten by bears.

Fortunately for Bob's friends as well as his art, he has lived long. Long enough to have proven his faith, enlarged his hope, and sharpened the unlikely optimism he has held since his youth.

Robert Rees's vision of the natural world—including its complications, disappointments, anxieties, and doubts—is at once joyous and profound, comprising facets of a single lens he brightens with insights either original or originally expressed.

Bob is an enthusiast, and there are ecstatic moments in his poems, moments larger than their envisioning, like Gerard Manley Hopkins shouting,

Look at the stars! look, look up at the skies!
O look at all the fire-folk sitting in the air!
The bright boroughs, the circle-citadels there!

Those are lines that may well have been written by Bob, infused at once by wonder and worship in which even the commonest moments are energized by the novelty he discovers in ordinary life, or made serious (but never solemn), recognizing that life is mixed, that events cannot be relied upon. The enthusiasms of the child Bob remembers being—a child whose life was complicated by misadventure and abuse—are tempered by the "long thoughts" of a wounded youth and the insights of a relentlessly inquiring adult. Now an octogenarian, Bob has spent more time than most wondering about both sides of the veil, but never doubting the happy resolution of life in death or the immediate and fundamental generosity of living.

Bob is eighty-two—older than Shelley survived; older even than Wordsworth who was thought "ancient" by contemporaries before he died at eighty; and while Frost merely permitted "Eden" as a poetic device, Bob believes it. That means he believes ours is a fallen world, but his poems discover in the complexity of that world fallen from grace the "opposition in things": a world made by God to refract both birth and death, virtue and corruption, youth and decay. But always there is a foreshadowing of a more perfect world to come.

While Bob's poems are colored by the American Romanticism of Whitman, they are deeply influenced by the Transcendentalism of Emerson, which is why his life and attitude are more the quiet, insightful, disagreement Emerson had with orthodoxy than the outright rebellion of Thoreau or the retreat into naturalism of Walden Pond. His poetry is pastoral, but shining behind the natural world is the Light of the World, and that light infuses Bob's poetry with anticipation.

Which is why if we were to define the poetry of Robert Rees as merely or principally pastoral, it would be a misdirection. Because his conversation with the natural world is a complication, not a direction. Not the complication of innocence confronted by experience as in William Blake, but of the natural as revealed and transformed by the supernatural, and the supernatural transcending nature (the unintentional) and infusing and defining the life force of love (the intentioned and animating force that, as Dylan Thomas suggests, "through the green fuse drives the flower....").

Life, love, loss, redemption, sacrifice, and even sin are of a single cloth for Bob, refractions of a beam of light emanating from its creator. Which is one of the reasons that in Bob's lyrical world there is a sense of place that may remind of nineteenth-century pastoral verse (his doctorate focused on Transcendentalists such as Emerson, Thoreau, Whitman, and Emily Dickinson). But this isn't the naïve geography of the English Romantics, nor the artificial hardship of New England communes. Nor yet the small towns and sidewalks that tethered Southern writers to a claustrophobic rural society.

The space Bob inhabits is a topography distinguished by mountains to climb and woods through which to walk as much as it is by literature, music, art, worship, and his unique joyousness. Paradoxically, what makes that joy uniquely his own is how unlikely were its beginnings in a childhood terrified by angry, abusive, alcoholic adults.

So, we are not surprised when we find separation and death in Bob's poems. What is surprising is that there is no graveyard in the poet. In "Waiting for Morning," for example, a poem about the death of his father, Bob, sitting in the early dawn of his father's last hours, sees not defeat or darkness but rather "a world ablaze with blossom," a world that awaits "some morning" when

> . . . my father will come,
> shouldering through earth, rising
> through new grass, strong as trees
> growing into the sun.

An image as alarming as it is inspiring, it joins a number of such moments to deny what may be the laziest criticism of Bob's poems: that they are only optimistic or naïve and sentimental. The universe of Bob's art is not a mindless ecstasy, but a serious response to what he perceives as the overarching confirmations of Nature and Nature's God. Confirmations that do not deny but encompass the tragic. "Elegy" speaks of the brutality of a fallen world in which we are condemned by the creatures we kill in our mad rush along the highways of modernism:

> These bruised deaths,
> jagged wounds of flesh— . . .
> sparrows and meadow larks ruptured
> in sunlight, swallows and owls torn
> from night, the million insects—
> carcasses frozen in sun, dried
> gourds of bones, parched scrolls of skin,
> casings of cicadas, husks of wasps,
> the iridescent wrecked wings of butterflies:
> our chronic feast of flies,
> our unholy harvest of crows.

Flies and crows. These are not merely literary allusions, but literally flies and crows. And, miraculously: love.

Undefeated by accepting the evidence of life's cruelty, Bob's vision of love expresses itself as anticipation, as exemplified by his love of his wife, of his children and grandchildren, of Christ, and of the world itself. However hard the moment, love is:

> like the heart-shaped
> morning glories climbing the stone wall . . .

or,

> psalms and praises [that]
> rise to fill the rounded arches [of a church]
> in a curve of love.

And because love of God and love of family are interchangeable in the poems, one leading Bob inevitably to the other, some of us—especially those of us who know Bob well—may be inclined to approach this collection as religious verse, and Bob probably would not be offended to have it described as a kind of worship.

But describing Bob's poetry as specifically religious—as "Christian" or "Mormon" or even as an anticipation of moral conclusions—again points us in a direction that is specifically rather than generally accurate, that is blind to the refraction. Because although his moral philosophy pronounces itself in his poems, Bob's poetry is not didactic; and his aesthetic is as much biographical as theological or eschatological. Nor is it more religious than musical, more experiential than literary, or more personal than universal in its reverence for this world and his confidence in a next world that will confirm the everlasting love, beauty, and confidence Bob has in all the evidences he has found of ultimate meaning.

It is that insistent belief in a moral world that communicates not only Bob's joy and anticipation but also his acceptance of disappointment and tragedy as natural and part of the good. Where there is tragedy, Bob does not suggest it can be explained or rationalized as redemptive. If we are to believe, we believe in spite of much in the world, even in spite of ourselves. As in "Morgenstern," a memorial for a forgotten Polish boy who died in the Holocaust:

> . . . and for all of Rachel's
> children whose six-pointed stars
> lie scattered among the forgotten fields of memory.

And "Aleppo," where a bewildered child lost among the ruined landscape of Syria suffers:

> Beneath her eyes
> bruised crescents,
> the mute curve of her mouth
> a rose petal.

Even in such suffering are the remnants of beauty and hope for redemption. As a child, Bob was lost for a long while before finding himself (or being found) in family, religion, and literature. Which may be part of why Bob has a particular affinity for children whose lives are defined by abandonment and abuse, as remembered in such poems as "Ona," "Indigoes of Darkness," and "Heart-Rate Variability." And desertion and despair as obliquely recalled in such poems as "The Face of War" and "Famine and Scarcity," where children are abandoned to the obscenities of war and famine.

The miracle of Bob's optimism is not only that it is, but that it is in spite of the world, in spite of evidence to the contrary, in spite of what we cannot justify or explain. Because Bob is certain, that in spite of everything, there is hope and faith and—most of all—love.

That confidence does not permit more than mourning the profound suffering, abandonment, abuse, and violence suffered by him and countless millions of other children. What he endured and they continue to endure might have resulted in a worldview of opposite negatives, preferring neglect to abuse, apathy to antipathy, oblivion to suffering. Instead, the abuse and abandonment he suffered as a child encouraged in Bob an ambition to discover life-affirming and eternal evidences, discovering not the narrow rejection of childhood as his truth but reaching his arms wide around a love that can ignite the heart's capacity for forgiveness; and through forgiveness, understanding and even enlightenment. Certainly redemption.

Which is why—unlike so much confessional poetry—Bob's poems do not resent even the most desperate moments of the physical world. When there is no food, there is vanilla-flavored snow, which Bob makes sound so good, one may misunderstand the deep tragedy of the moment:

> I don't know if she kissed me or
> touched my cheek,
> but I remember
> the smell of vanilla,
> the taste of cold.

And a later poem about his mother's abandonment of him and his brother and sister when Bob was eight. Recalling that experience while in his seventies, he wrote,

> When we came home she wasn't there,
> and she never came back. . . .
> I keep wondering, could she have imagined
> that all these years later
> we would still be waiting?

Biographical criticism is flawed by its tendency to equivalency. But Bob's art is so counterintuitive to his childhood as to make it more miraculous than likely.

When Jesus promised his disciples peace, he made a disclaiming caveat: the peace to which he referred—and joy and hope and love—was not going to be what they expected: a single, bright, shiny light; but a refraction of that light into many and divergent and confusing instances. His is not the uncomplicated version of serenity promised by religion or the success or "fulfillment" promised by "self-actualization." His promise—and the promise in the poems of Robert Rees—is of meaning that transcends the disappointment of the self, and of love that transcends suffering and even death.

Perhaps that complication—that childhood and the peace and hope we look to proceed from it—is the intersection of the pastoral/theological/biographical influence that threads its way through Bob's lovely and sometimes terrifying poems, stitching together points of pigment as in a Seurat painting, each point more beautiful for being more significant than itself, each color shaded by every other color draining our eyes of color, each point fulfilled by the prism of the final art.

A prism refracting white light into its component colors at once reveals the fact of light while confusing the fact of pigment. The same combination of hue that brightens the world with light darkens the canvas with an increasing lack of clarity. To see and hear Bob's poems, one must look beyond the garden, beyond the first impression, beyond the color or the colors to the source of the light.

But in this age of digital art, atonal music, doubt believed to be superior to faith, despair more realistic than hope, proofs of The Fall more available than evidences of redemption, does an eighty-year-old poet promoting salvation have anything to tell us, anything that will help us more to feel or better to understand? For me, that's a mischievous and rhetorical question, but one I intended to ask Bob before completing this unnecessary introduction of these essential and lovely poems.

So, long past my deadline, with no more time to procrastinate, I called to worry Bob into an answer.

He was not home and out of cell range, feeding malnourished children in Peru and climbing Machu Picchu.

EXPERIENCE

Uncle Robert

passed through the front door
late last Tuesday evening
and headed up the road.

Just before he left,
while he was taking a long
afternoon nap, perhaps
sensing he might be going,
I slipped into his pocket a
measuring tape,
    pocket knife,
    and just enough change
to make it to the Maine turnpike.

Today, the white chairs on the front
porch are empty. The straight
bleached boards, running from shadow
to light, lead, like the planes in a
Renaissance painting, to some
diminishing point where
sun joins sea and sky.
The porch frames the light
yet opens to heaven in such a way
that I cannot tell if light is
    pouring in or
    flowing out,
it is so bright.

Heart Mountain
(Wyoming Relocation Camp, 1942)

At the Japanese American National Museum
a pile of stones
no bigger than my thumb, each
with a single kanji,
found buried at Heart Mountain.
Each stone names something of the world—
horse, river, flower, snow,
kimono, sword, blossom, death—
piled like a mountain
in a bonsai landscape.

No one knows why.

I see her there walking the fence
and empty river bed that runs
through the camp. She bends or squats
to pick up stones,
choosing each
before placing it in her pocket.
As she walks, she thinks of her son
buried in France,
her husband sick in the barracks
with no medicine, her home in Fresno
inhabited by strangers, and her daughter
whose dreams lie dead along the San Joaquin.

She dreams herself of a village outside Kyoto,
the peonies in her father's garden, and
plum blossoms on Mt. Fuji.
She fears she will go mad here
where summer dust blows through the walls
and in winter no fire can keep them warm.

At night in the tarpaper rooms
where they are prisoners, she
names the world and its parts—
earth, apple, jade, moon,
sun, dog, table, heaven.

Each day she picks up new stones.

The Dancing Beggar of London

I saw him at Leicester Square
then two nights later at Piccadilly;
tonight he's at King's Cross.

Flesh like moss on ashen trees,
legs and arms absurdly akimbo,
he dances to his tambourine,
a comic Christ, a ghostly harlequin.

Coins drop into his sack—
stones tossed down an ancient well
where no water waits nor circles move.

At Chekhov's play, actors move with
grace and speak their lines
on a well-set stage: "Dear Sisters,
if we live a little longer, perhaps we will
come to know why . . . "

A Mirror for Josephine Miles

Arms, bandaged branches;
feet, twists of burled walnut;
draped in a green gown, she speaks
of *The Mirror for Magistrates*—
crowns cracked and cracking.

Mornings, she crawls to the mirror like
the woman in Wyeth's landscape
leaning against the winter grasses and
looks in the silvered circle where she sees
a wren of a woman at an oaken table,
a vase of sweet Williams at her side, new poets
at her feet, and *that* woman looks back
into eyes from which arise a sweep
of swans, wheeling and careening
over darkening trees, their perfect wings
catching early sun.

Elegy

I ran back hoping it wasn't alive.
In the road nothing but a delicate
pile of intestines giving off
steam. In the ditch a mottled body
angled among dandelions.
All the way to Wyoming the car
smelled of excrement and blood.

South of the Tetons, a prickly
bulge alongside the road,
and further on, two black-tailed
jack rabbits clumped in bunchgrass
like welts of sod. At Owens Valley
a malodorous smudge; in the parking
lot at Old Faithful the small wound
of a meadow mouse; ten miles north
of Yellowstone a dead buffalo
hunched in the ditch like
a furred boulder.

These bruised deaths,
jagged wounds of flesh—
antelope and elk mangled on the roadway,
snakes broken on the tarmac, ponderous
tortoises cracked along black rivers,
sparrows and meadowlarks ruptured
in sunlight, swallows and owls torn
from night, the million insects—
carcasses frozen in sun, dried
gourds of bones, parched scrolls of skin,
casings of cicadas, husks of wasps,
the iridescent wrecked wings of butterflies:

our chronic feast of flies,
our unholy harvest of crows.

New World

—*For Barry Lopez*

The aviaries of Tenochtitlan
held the sky's amazement
in their ribbed worlds—white egrets,
fierce accipiters, rainbow-
colored parrots, vermillion fly-
catchers, copper-tailed
trogons, blue-throated
hummingbirds, summer tanagers,
and great blue herons.

The Spaniards heard the cantatas
of birdsong—eerie, high-pitched
arias, deep-throated
harmonies floating over
the canals and gardens—
and wondered . . .

                              then
at Cortez' command they torched
the pavilions of
melody, burning
them to the ground.

Hearing the hysterical cries,
the terror of stunted flight,
the stench of singed feathers,
what newer world
did they imagine?

The Cedars of Lebanon

There is nothing in Lebanon.
We are playing in our own blood.
  —A Maronite monk (1988)

Across a shattered street, a Muslim groom lifts
the train of his Christian bride as he steps
over broken glass, old tires, and piles of rubblestone.
Her face is a dark rose in this ravaged landscape.

The guns are silent for this small repose.

Here Phoenicians made their alphabet for lovers
to speak their marriage vows and death
be called by its endless names. At nearby Cana
Jesus turned water into wine
at a wedding feast of friends.

Today there are no miracles, just these
fugitive angels fleeing the world while
pigs and wild dogs root in the rubble.

Each spring the waters of the Adonis flow
from limestone caverns deep in the heart
of Mount Lebanon. As they descend
though rust hills, the waters turn red, flowing,
as the old story goes, from wounds torn
in the flesh of the beautiful youth by Ares
disguised as a wild boar.

On this day when Adonis blossoms
adorn the wedding bed, Aphrodite holds
her dying love as her tears
speed the crimson river to the sea.

Karbala

My Muslim student:
among
twenty million
flocking to
the Valley of Paradise:
"I felt like I was
walking on sky."

Melancholia

*"Watch what happens sometimes when a young child is allowed to just
have his or her feelings. The feelings usually run their course and the
child comes full circle."*
—*Tobin Hart,* The Secret Spiritual World of Children

"I'm sad.
It feels like the whole world
is inside me," says
my five-year-old grandson, naming
the invisible darkness
of heart,
the black bile
of soul,
that oppresses
like an anvil sky.

This ancient affliction,
grief gathering to greatness,
anomie the enemy
of King Saul, Jeremiah,
Hamlet and Camus,
of Woolf and Styron.

Dowland sang it darkly
and Dickinson,
oppressed by winter light,
felt a funeral in her brain:
generations
descending to darkness.

———

Such sadness of soul reaches
even the heavens
where the despondent angels,
ungladdened by rainbow or sunburst,
brood with alchemical lassitude.

Even God,
who sang the whole world into being,
when the weight of history
presses down, when
sequestered hates
and serial annihilations
lean everything backward to chaos
and no flood or fire
can extinguish
the darkness.

For some it seems an eternity.
For others, it passes
like the going of a great storm,
as with my grandson,
who says,
hours later,
"I'm okay now—
the whole world
is outside me."

Easter

My grandson, ten,
hates the rain,
as he does this Sunday morning
when dark clouds bring the sky down.
He announces he is not going to church:
"I'm anti-Christian."
His mom says,
"Nevertheless, get dressed.
It's Easter."
"You know I don't believe
all that gobbledygook,"
he replies.
"Don't forget to tie your shoes," she says.

At church I see him play
with the baby
in the next row then snuggle
against his mother,
solid as faith.

In the foyer following church he
bows to touch the face of a
Down syndrome child
with exquisite echoing
of her slow small vowels.

On the way home,
we see a dead raccoon.
He asks to stop
so we can bury it.
He's quiet until we reach home then says,

"I hope it gets resurrected."

———

Famine and Scarcity

My grandson, seven,
head bent over his crustless peanut-
butter and honey sandwich,
bowl of grapes
and cup of juice,
says these very words:
"Heavenly Father,
bless that there will be no war, famine
or scarcity in the land."
And I wonder where this
pocket prophet heard such a biblical phrase
and how in his Sabbath year
he seems to understand.

On the evening news I see
bone piles, the vultures of war,
and beneath a tangled bush in Africa
a woman holding her ghost child—
a collapsed puppet.

At night I say my clichés
for the wrecked and wretched of the world
who speak holy words
to the sky's vast darkness.

Universe

In the bedroom of my one-week-old grandson,
a blue planet circled by blue rings hangs
from the ceiling. Beneath it a crescent moon
surrounded by twelve translucent stars
and below it all a shooting star.
This mobile heaven with its galaxies,
quarks and supernovas, stands
for a universe contracting and collapsing.

In my arms another universe,
that will expand infinitely.

The Bridge

Dropping from the Sierras,
we stopped to swim in the American River.
Our Scouts and Explorers set off
from the bridge feet first,
banshees cannonballing
into the stream.

Ricky Adams, golden boy
of that Gold Country,
was among them, jumping
over and over.

Did he remember any of this in the blue-
blood cold of yesterday's dawn when,
darkness crowding his heart, he jumped
from the Golden Gate Bridge and
fell two hundred feet into the Bay?

For a moment did the thrill
of that other fall cross his mind,
the ring of boyssong reach his ears,
the catch of breath fill his heart
as he fell into darkness?

In that instant did he remember
a time when boys could free-
fall through space into a timeless stream
        and rise to do it again
        and again, as if forever?

19

Blackbirds
(Kaunas, Lithuania 1994)

On Christmas morning
at the Kauno Vaiku Pensionatas,
twelve of the two hundred orphans
have been left behind. The others
have gone with aunts and uncles,
grandparents and friends, or the
faithful sisters of Caritas.

Outside the snow crunches under our feet
as cold blows from the Neris River.
As I look toward the sky, I see
three great trees filled with hundreds
of fat black birds.

A Girl in Aleppo

In the New York *Times,*
a photograph of a girl
nine or ten,
dark eyes, short brown hair,
cyan scarf,
carmine-red blouse under
a white and teal jumper
and string of plastic pearls.
Beneath her eyes
bruised crescents,
the mute curve of her mouth
a rose petal.

For Anne Frank

Alone in her room, I touch
the walls she touched, gaze at
images she clipped from magazines
and books and pinned to her walls:
her gallery of kings and queens,
movie stars and artists, drawings
of lush landscapes—fragments
of her imagined world.

I watch her gliding
over the wooden floor,
waltzing with Ray Milland.
The dance ended,
he bows as
Robert Stack steps in.
Rudy Vallee waits against the wall.

She dances all night, her golden
gown silently brushing the floor as she spins.

No. 263 Prinsegracht, Amsterdam

Through a small space
in the blackened window
she watched the world change:
leaves falling into the canal,
brown and yellow dreams that floated
to the sea; snow that buried her
songs through nights and dark days;
bright tulips and birdsong
in the hot-house garden of her mind;
the sweltering days of bees-sound,
breezeless suffocation of desire.

Beautiful as Susanna,
doomed as
Rachael's children,
a memory
for madness.

Morgenstern

I am given an identification card:
"David Morgenstern,
born in Kaluszyn, Poland, 1935,"
the year of my birth.
Inside, the photo of a boy of four or five
with angelic face and sad eyes.
It is the only image of him
that survives.

It says, "For the dead *and* the living
we must bear witness."

In a few weeks we will sing Bach's
Wie schön leuchtet der Morgenstern
for our Christmas service.
For this unfortunate boy, there was no mercy
beaming from afar on the machinery of extermination,
no hosts of heaven rejoicing in the dark Polish forests.

On this December day I carry his image,
bearing it though the annals of the unbearable,
witnessing to the living and the dead
that this David was once a morning star
whose brief light fell into the silence of history.

Carrying his photo like an emblem of the Eucharist,
I remember him, as I remember that
Son of David nailed to a tree whose star
still shines over the bent world and whose heart
still breaks, for this forgotten boy and for all of Rachel's
children whose six-pointed stars
lie scattered among the forgotten fields of memory.

The Face of War

"That which seemed its head . . ."
—*John Milton,* Paradise Lost

On a sunny day in Basra or Baghdad,
a child's face is fractured beyond
anything human, as if God
shaping an image of himself
had dropped the clay on stones:
eyeless and a bloody rupture
where a mouth had been.

The child's face gone
and with it all we count
of ourselves so long
out of the arroyos and savannahs:
our songs and sonnets,
cathedrals and cantatas,
our skyscrapers and spaceships,
our science and psalms—

are nothing now.

ABANDONED

Ona

That's her, standing somewhat stiffly
with the others in Rye, Colorado,
the year of the Great Crash.
Her cousin Mavis is there too,
third girl from the left.
She looks more poised
than my mother, who stands
in a corner, her passive face
lit like a cameo.

By this time her father was already fondling
her breasts, which are just beginning to
show beneath the cotton middy she wears
with the sailor collar. He caught her
in the barn where they milked the cows
and in the creamery when she made butter.

At fourteen she was sent to live
with her Aunt Ida in Cortez, making
the trip over Wolf Creek Pass
the darkest day of the year.
Four years later she and my father ran
away to Monticello to get married.
When she was seven months pregnant
with me, her second child,
she drank a bottle of blue poison.

Her second husband shot a woman
then cut his own throat with a razor.
Her third husband died in a fire
a year after he raped her. For
a while she lived with an ex-
convict and then married a guy
named Birchell O. Eden.
Her fifth marriage was to her
own daughter's third husband.

Not long before she died of heart
failure and he was killed by a car
while crossing the street in Delta,
the old man was still pressing her.

The other boys and girls in the picture
look innocent, expectant, dreaming
of girlfriends, boyfriends, basketball
and dresses for the school prom.
My mother alone casts a shadow
on the pastoral backdrop hung clumsily
by the photographer, who cannot see
what she knows and can never tell
anyone, especially her classmates
standing so full of promise before
the black, one-eyed box.

Pearl Harbor

"Those are pearls that were his eyes."
—The Tempest

Beneath these waters
their bones in repose,
buried
in an instant
by bombs and torpedoes.
At that moment, in a small Arizona town,
my father
fresh from milking
sits down for a late breakfast
and listens to the radio.
We are too young to
understand
but recognize a fear
we know from dreams.
Later their voices erupt
strafing the night.
She begs him not to go.
Soon he sails
from San Francisco
for islands of death
across the Pacific.

In the museum I look up
at the small plane
suspended from
the ceiling
and remember the story:
A bomber
heading straight
for my father's small ship
at the last moment,
changes course
to hit a nearby destroyer.

There is nothing he can do
while eternity is suspended in time.

My Father sees blood and fire
on the water,
a severed arm,
Images that no whisky
will wash away.

Looking at the placid sea,
I bow my head
for all that unfolded
from that day
when I was six
and the world
twisted on its axis
to this.

Heart-rate Variability

My baseline begins in Durango
when I am seven. Snow
the night before. White sheets
billowing the sky. Mother sends us
to scoop away flecks of coal dust
and bring the milkyblue snow
just below the surface.

Our father writes he is transporting
soldiers up the beach at Iwo Jima.
He looks up to see a Kamakazi.
There is nothing he can do
as the pilot hits a destroyer
a thousand yards away.

Standing on tiptoe, Mom takes down vanilla
and sugar and fetches a bottle of milk
from the front porch, the frozen cream
risen above the mouth
like a thick, white mushroom.
Together we make snow ice cream,
the only kind we can afford.

As canons and rockets rain down from Mt. Sarabachi,
our father sees bodies all over the beach
and more floating in the water,
the incarnadine pools spreading outward.
He thinks of his sons and wonders
if he will see them again.

We help Mom pick apples from the tree
in our backyard and wrap them in newspaper.
Billy and I carry them to the cellar.
We eat a few and hide the cores
in the corner.

Caught in a typhoon, our father's ship
rises to the sky then falls eighty feet,
crashing into the sea.
In the hold, he prays
that God will spare his life.

We slice cabbage heads into a barrel.
When it is nearly full, Mom pours in brine.
Sauerkraut for winter which also
goes to the cellar. I cut my hand;
when she pours mercurochrome,
the pink red bleeding through the gauze
leaves a trail across the floor.

Our father writes that a bomb
has sent shrapnel into his head and legs.
He is transported to a hospital in Guam
and later in Oceanside doctors cut a line
from the base of his skull to his spine
extracting pieces of metal. He sends his love.

One day our mother leaves with a boyfriend
and doesn't come back. We are alone in the house
for weeks before the authorities put us
in a foster home.

Our father gets special leave from the hospital.
One day he knocks at the door.

Cold Sweet

Although she hadn't wanted me born,
when I was, I suppose
she suckled me,
holding me against her
as mothers do.
Perhaps
she rocked me, our heartbeats
searching for one another.
She may have held me
against the warm curve
of her belly when we slept,
breathing as one.

And yet there are no memories,

except

a blue porcelain bowl she hands me
to fill with snow
after scooping away the coal dust.

In the kitchen
we mix sugar and vanilla.
She places a spoonful
of cold sweet
in my mouth.

I don't know if she kissed me or
touched my cheek,
but I remember
the smell of vanilla,
the taste of cold.

Indigos of Darkness

There isn't a place
in this world that doesn't

sooner or later drown
in the indigos of darkness
—Mary Oliver

When we came home she wasn't there,
and she never came back.

We charged food at the store next door,
mostly candy and soda pop.

When we ran out of clean shirts,
we wore pajama tops to school

then stayed home
when kids teased us.

Seventy years later, I remember
sleeping in her bed

smelling her absence,
cradled in her indentation,

holding one another against
the bruised blue darkness.

What did we do all day—
Billy who was nine, me seven,

and Janet four? For two weeks
no one came, and then the police.

We were put in a home. The courts
sent for our father who was in the South Pacific,

but it took months for the letters to catch up
with him in a Navy hospital in Oceanside.

I remember I kept saying,
"My Daddy is in the war and he's coming

to get me," but I wasn't sure he would.
I keep wondering, could she have imagined

that all these years later we would
still be waiting?

Waiting for Morning
(Easter Sunday, 1984)

His winter eyes blank,
the thin brush of his mind
tumbles in his dreams.

Out the window I watch
torrents of rain wash the day
as lightning divides the night.

On the way to the hospital
boxwood and cherry, lilac,
sumac, apple, pear, and purple-
blue morning glories climbing everywhere—
all the trees, vines and bushes
expanding, exploding
into light.

Unsure of this place, my father
opens his eyes, speaks
my name, then slips back
into Lethe's stream.

Each spring Christ calls
all the world's flowers and wild weeds;
calls rivers and rivulets from hills, bees
and butterflies from blossoms.

Some morning my father will come,
shouldering through earth, rising
through new grass, strong as trees
growing into the sun.

Black Flower

Her body was cold, nearly
frigid in the small room
set aside for such matters.

He watched as they threaded
her arms and legs through
the undergarment with its
archaic symbols.

Then the robe, yellow from disuse,
followed by the apron, its green leaves
darkened around the edges
and the soiled sash the sisters
tied neatly at her waist.

After the viewing, when they
had placed the cap on her head and
pulled the veil over her face, and everyone
had retreated to the chapel, he stood alone
looking at her one last time.

Before he closed the casket,
he took the flat black flower
he found pressed in her bible
these fifty years, and placed it
over her heart.

Black Handkerchief

Lying on the table,
he was as handsome
as the day he had taken her
through the veil.

Now his body was impotent,
his anger veiled in death.

She saw his nakedness
one last time before the high priests
dressed the body for burial.

After the garments, robe, and
sash, the bright leaved apron
and the stiff white cap,
she asked the bishop

for a few minutes alone with the man
she had been sealed to for time
and eternity. She did not

kiss him as she had intended,
but looked one last time
at his rigid face, then, slipping
the black lace handkerchief from her sleeve,
she placed it over his face and quietly
closed the casket.

CHINA POEMS

Listening in China

On the road to the Grand Buddha
near Chengdu, workers chisel
red stone blocks.

On the banks of the Changjiang
just outside Chongquing
men with hammers chip road rocks.

On the cliffs down river by
Anping, young women
carve deep stone steps:

Chinese work music.

Liu Shahe

His speech makes measured
music in the old Sichuan dialect.
He quotes Confucius, Walt
Whitman and Li Po then
tells the American writer
her name sounds like pearls
dropping in a dish—
Hong-ting-ting.

During the long darkness Liu
shaped hard wood with plane and saw,
fashioned cabinets tight as tombs.
As witness to his children,
he wrote poems in the night.
When the Red Guards came he
burned the scraps of paper,
and tossed the ashes in the wind.

These days he stays home,
writes old style poems—
"traces of the saw tooth's edge—
cipher of awl and auger"—
and complains about young poets
writing crazy verse.

"My children no longer read my
poems," he says, "They just
rock and roll . . .

Rolling Stones."

Yellow Crane Tower

Watch the confluence of the rivers
from the top of the Tower,
and words will flow like the
ochre waters of the Yangtze,
so the story goes.

By the time our boat lands, it's late.
Monks guard the Tower gate
and Buddhist bells ring
as trains run in the night.

At the Qingachuan Hotel, the poet,
Xi She, who for twenty years
dreamed the rivers from a
pig farm outside Chengdu, says,
"Never mind. The top of the hotel
gives a better view and the effect
 is just the same."

Next morning I ride the elevator
to the top then scramble up
a flight of stairs to the observation
deck. Through a window in the door
I look toward the rivers,
but the glass is dirty so all I see

is my own face.

Patterns

—for Gary Snyder

At the silk factory in Suzhou

> young women in gray smocks
> muse over French fashion books
> dreaming up patterns

Across a passage way
pigskin and fish dry in rows
weaving wave shadows on the factory roof

> A young man in blue over and over
> pushes and pulls back red dye
> with the silk-screen print roller

Down an alley
row on row of red canna lilies
decorate the factory steps

> The drying machine spills out silk
> looping and billowing
> in white canvas bins

In the loom of a broken window
a spider spins filaments
threading afternoon sun.

Echoes of the Han Shan Bell
(with Gary Snyder and Allen Ginsburg,
Suzhou, China, 30 October 1984)

Gary Snyder gives a copy of
Cold Mountain Poems to the old priest
at Han Shan temple:
"This book has finally
come home."

The bell sound in his heart,
he reads Zhang Ji at Feng Bridge
and writes a poem.

Sitting on Maple Bridge,
Allen hears it too
and writes his own.

On the train back to Shanghai
Masa recalls learning Zhang Ji
in a country school outside Kyoto
and remembers every line.

Tai Chi in Xian

An old man moves in morning,
a great blue heron awakening—
his coat sleeves riffle, wings
slowly shaking off night.

The painted eyebrow thrushes
rejoice in the almond trees

He balances on one leg,
a crane, arms and hands
tucked tight then spread wide,
cradling light.

The ochre-colored bailing
chorus from the locusts

Left hand embraces tiger,
right plucks the sparrow's
tail. As feathers fall
to ground, he circles
to the mountain.

The blue-throated canaries
exult among the poplars

His meditation complete,
a blue-black egret
lifts from the Junghe River
to jubilate the sky.

Spring Comes to the Ming Tombs

The persimmons are gone—
soft suns, astringent skins,
sweet slippery meat that held
summer past first frost.

The trees are still bare,
though sparrows and finches—
singers of early green—
keep chorus there.

Along the road
peasants sell Chinese pears,
sallow skinned from cellars
dark as tombs.

Beyond the vermilion walls
acacias scatter buds
and the forsythia blossoms
in tiny yellow butterflies.

Here where royalty once rode
in golden coaches, stone
horses and elephants keep vigil.

LOVE

Sand

He explained he would be gone
for a few weeks
but would see her in his office
when he returned.
"I'm going to the beach."
She looked at him
with an absence
that had grown
these past months.
"Ramsar."
He waited for more.
"Is that in Iran?"
"Come to the orchard in spring.
There is light . . .
in the pomegranate flowers."

A poem?
Nothing. Then again
"Ramsar."

"I'm going to the beach," he repeated.
I'll be back soon."
He saw the hourglass of her mind,
the grains
flowing slowly to the center,
then falling
to make a miniature mountain.

"Do you remember the beach?"
Again a long pause.
"There is a kind of music there."
He saw the ocean in her eyes.
"Can I bring you something?"
"Sand."

Late Spring

Lying on our backs
looking into the green galaxy
of the mandarin tree with it hundreds
of small orange planets,
we dream a world
without clocks or computers,
just poetry
and love,
as the sun descends
on a late afternoon in May.

Meanwhile,
Time
sits in the Starbucks over
on Fourth Street
sipping
his double Caffé Latte
acting as if we have
all the time
in the world.

Poems

(after W. C. Williams)

1. Plums

This gnarled, moss-covered tree,
barren for decades,
has fruited an abundance of plump
purple black. I picked
a handful for you—then ate them
on the way home, otherwise
I would have put them in the fridge
and written you a poem about
their sweetness and how
they are as ripe as love itself.

2. Cat

Soft as silk
slipping from a woman's
body, our cat
poured her black
into my glass
to lap the last level
of milk. In the beveled
panes her eyes grew large,
her nose contracted
and then, as simply,
she withdrew
and licked the drops of cream
from her whiskers.

Shade

"Had the price of looking been blindness, I would have looked."
—Ralph Ellison, "Battle Royal"

When I was twelve and
delivered the *Arizona Republic*
along the slow streets of Reid's Addition,
one evening, at dusk, as I leaned
my bike against the white picket fence
at Jackie Evan's house and
went to collect from his mom,
like Susanna stepping from her bath,
she walked toward
the large front window, slowly
reached up and just as slowly
lowered the shade.

I stood stock still, collection book in hand,
watching the blind descend, past
her long brown hair, her enormous
breasts and alabaster skin, past
the dark delta, where
my mind stopped.

Seventy years later I see her,
framed by the window, the last rays
of sun glazing her body
as the shade descends.

Love in the Sun

I look at the woman on the cover of *The Sun*.
Wearing a summer print dress, she holds a
sleeping child in her arms
like Mary in Michelangelo's Pietá.
A leg is drawn underneath the child
as she sits on a wooden chair.
Even in this moment
burdens overwhelm her.
I would hold her
as she holds this child,
with pity and love
in the sun.

Gene at Wilder Beach
(September 2001)

Blessed
are those who listen
when no one is left to speak.
—Linda Hogan

Were you here,
we would talk about the straight seam
that divides sea from sky,
and how the world is not like that at all.
We would talk about these caves,
how the one, resplendent with ferns,
seems like a flowering heart,
and how the other, which the sea
has washed to blackness, is like the mysteries
we sometimes explored. We would talk
of falling towers and civilizations and how
in dark times we hold poetry in our hearts.

But you are not here, and so I listen alone
to the sea's soft sibilants, the pelican's
cry, the liquid splash of dolphins.

An enormous log washed against the back of the cove
by winter storms stood tall in the Santa Cruz mountains,
drinking underground rivers and reaching toward the sun.
It too speaks through its multitude of markings—
curved lines, strange scribblings, deep scars,
words of bark and bugs, voices of rivers and seas—
the runed and ruined language of the world.

Tonight is for You
(Concertgebouw, Amsterdam, 1956)

Isaac Stern tunes his violin
for rehearsal of the concerto
he'll soon play.
Having read the diary and
visited the rooms
where Beethoven was unheard
those long silent months,
he thinks about
the daughter he may
someday have, whose name
he has already chosen—
"Shira"—("My song").

Violin in hand,
he looks
at the open case,
the dark-haired girl's photo
pinned inside:
"Tonight is for you."

Angels

Lying on the lawn
at Magdalen Gardens,
we see the cerulean sky
heavy with white hydrangea-clouds.
As children,
we imagined a world in clouds:
sheep, ghosts, snowmen,
white smoke billowing from chimneys
and locomotives,
and once a white stallion
rearing on its hind legs,
but today
looking heavenward,
holding your hand
and the scent of roses in the air,
I see only
angels.

NATURE

Wild Turkeys

Marine headlands
before dawn,
our grandchildren,
troubled by dreams,
come to bed.
Outside a bobolink
awakens the world
and from some place in the hills
the gargle-gobble-gurgle
of wild turkeys.

Frogs disappearing
in wetlands,
bees and butterflies
gone to who knows?
The great ice sheets
sloughing into seas,
lions dying of distemper
on the Serengeti,
elephants
wilding in jungles—
the ever-vanishing
wilderness.

This systolic and diastolic
pulse of creation:
the downward pull of destruction,
decay and death;
the thermodynamic depletion of energy;
the counter, outward,
upward thrust of life.

Loud and far wild turkeys
strut in the half light,
feathers fanned,
fantastically announcing spring.

April

All along
Pacific Coast Highway,
California poppies
in the median:
small schools of garibaldi
swimming in a Sargasso Sea
of wild mustard and new grass.

Praise

Up King's Creek,
a royal four-foot snake
absorbing summer sun,
its black and white bands
dividing the world
with absolute certainty.
Even my approaching
does not disturb it.
Such steadfastness,
and clear cleavage:
no ambiguity, nuance or uncertainty—
a fixed zebra line
drawn in the sand.

Rainbow-winged butterflies,
harlequin dragonflies,
paint the air;
spotted salamanders
swim in sunlight—
all things moving to uncertain tides
and itinerant dreams.

Glory be to God for multiplicity
and mystery, for subtlety and shade,
ambiguity and enigma—
of stars that stipple space, the slow
gravitation of glaciers,
oceans that move the moon:
this tangle of mind and
hive of heart,
of sun into black and
night into white.

Gilead

The sugar maple burns
against the sky,
flowering among sage and juniper,
cedar and pine,
as if it alone drank summer sun,
mirroring in final flame
that golden circumstance.
Its fire is the heart
of the mountain that lights
the trees of all the wood:

    the florescent tree
    at the edge of Eden
    where cherubim still circle;
    the incandescent bush
    where Moses trembled
    when the Word bound his bones;
    Lehi's luminous tree,
    whose fruit divide the night
    like ripe moons;
    the fresh-cut evergreen,
    its colored candles
    swaddling starlight;
    the broken branch
    where the light was nailed,
    and all the leaves turned red;
    the golden bough of Byzantium,
    among whose fine hammered leaves
    the holy birds still sing;
    and, at the end, the timeless tree
    reflected in the river,
    its twelve fruit the balm of nations—

and at once all the trees of the field
clap their hands and rejoice,
sending their roots along the stream,
their foliage ever green
against the dying year.

Honored by an Award in Poetry by the Association of Mormon Letters, 1980; Sun-
stone *(6:1), January-February 1981; Reprinted in* Harvest (Salt Lake City: Signatur
Books, 1989).

Burning Bush

The Japanese maple
in our front yard,
each leaf a tongue of fire, and
from the ground
revenants of blazing words
sing in autumn air
Holy, Holy, Holy.

.

I hear his voice from the Mesozoic ginko,
its strange leaves
lighting the tree with golden
butterflies,
and from the back orchard,
each apple a pome
of praise.

Annus Mirabilis

The barest buds in the bay tree
on Carrera Street;
the bees sing in
the new year;
the magnolia's
purple and white blossoms; and
wild turkeys,
their nacreous wings
enfolding the year's dense prism—
seem-spring.

Morning Glory

Every day this spring
I watched the hillside
beyond our front yard
turn imperceptibly
from green
to gray
to gold—
in morning light
and evening sun.
Now early summer, against the
wheat-colored grass
I see more clearly:
California poppies,
purple larkspur,
starflowers,
wild lilac—and
morning glories climbing
the ancient oaks.

At Ring Mountain Wetlands

A lone egret
white as Christ
stands stock still
in rust and ochre weeds,
the bayonet
of its beak poised.
Suddenly, it rises and
floats with angel wings
over the wetlands,
alighting further off
to resume as
Death's silent sentinel.

Jacaranda

Almost agapanthus,
nearly ageratum,
this imaginary blue.

Brown-plated pita pods—
brittle blue-blossom
seed pockets.

A week's anger—
under blue umbrella trees.
I touch your hand.

In the sculpture garden
Miro's dolphin watches
green trees fashion blue.

Late for class,
I walk barefooted
on purple-blue carpets.

The evergreen gathers
blossoms all day:
spring Christmas tree.

An old woman:
a single Jacaranda blossom
in her hair.

Lavender-blue rain
all April: ponds with-
out fish or frogs.

In the emerald Amazon
a sea of yellow jacarandas
more astonishing than blue.

Arbolitos con sus
flores azules:
lavanda floreando.

Jacarandas bloom
all over Watts: flecks
of Rodia's Towers.

Final exams:
one blossom left
on the tree.

In the Valley, purple-
blue trumpet-flower trees
among orange groves.

Mix mazarin and mauve
on black branches:
a sky garden flowers.

All the jacarandas
bare of blossom
long way 'til May.

Falling

The week I fell down the cellar steps,
our black oak fell in the night,
crashing in my dreams.
This morning, a vacant sky, a ruined chancel.

Cherry and Chestnut,
Swiss Stone, Ponderosa Pine,
Mountain Ash, Maple,
the blue blooming Jacaranda
in the sculpture garden,
the Liquid Elm at the courtyard
and the Birch by the Baptist church.

Beetles, beavers, bark rot;
hatchets, chain saws, double-bladed axes;
canker, ring rot, gall rust.

Laburnum and Laurel,
Eucalyptus, Sycamore,
Persimmon, Pomegranate,
Rosewood, Sandalwood.

Angiosperm, gymnosperm,
deciduous and evergreen,
leaves, fronds, branches, boughs,
twigs, needles, flowers, sprigs—
falling.

Needle blight, slime flux, oak wilt;
tsunami, wind storms, avalanches;
browntail moths, scarlet oak sawflies.

The new-sprung, new-leafed
saplings in the Blue Ridge Mountains,
seedlings of the Amazon.

The ariel-rooted Banyan,
the heavily-vined Mangrove,
the poison Pencil Tree,
Tropical Teak, Mahogany.

Bacteria, viruses, herbicide;
hemlock scale borer, spanworm, heart rot;
and the multiple destructions of war.

Even the Giant Sequoia
its canopy among stars,
the Bristle Cone Pine,
the Maidenhair Ginko,
its eternal leaves unfolding,
and these Coastal Redwoods,
alive since Christ—
must fall.

Yeats's golden bough,
Lehi's moon-fruited branches,
Buddha's Bodhi Tree,
the clonal Quaking Aspen
of the Uinta Range,
and that first perennial
at the heart of the Garden,
its flaming angel,
its crimson fruit.

Sun Seeds

A star in the Monoceros constellation
explodes
with the light of million suns,
luminous as the heart of God.

On this bright Sunday morning
in the Santa Cruz Mountains,
a lone persimmon, heavy with small suns,
each gestating sun-seeds
in astringent darkness.
I pick one and taste
its acidic sweetness.

That luminous star in the sky,
light echoing and radiance ricocheting
off hot and cool red stars,
spherical layers of dust and gas,
is also endless seeds
and blossoms.

That Moment

It was as if
a dark-edged angel
had pulled back
the curtain
on a new universe—
stars untethered from
obsidian,
galaxies burning
within galaxies,
planets careening,
meteors falling
like Lucifers into
expanding darkness,
illuminating
everything,
including the
vast
invisible
void.

Turning

A large persimmon tree
in the Santa Cruz Mountains
filled with starlings—
glossy green black passerines,
their chorus a jangling
of sleigh bells.

On the ground a multitude
of decaying suns
slough back to earth
sending light down and down
to rise in another year's
hard round fruit.

This world's turning:
from bright orange to burnt umber,
from terra sienna to cinnamon,
from astringent to sweet,
from branch to ground,
root to flower to fruit.

And on this winter day,
my heart's turning,
from darkness to sunfire:

the night's circumference
traducing to light.

Forgotten Birds

"Sleep is not death
but forgotten birds."
—David Hoag

1

The black-cassocked crow
broods in the eucalyptus
where blood-red umbellates
breathe out the odor of camphor.
As the graves grow green
and spring missiles its
multitudinous wings,
his shadow falls and
falls and
further falls
over the grasses,
over the greening,
beyond the growing.

2

Listening to kites
I hear all along
the long string
the wind vibrating,
its wild hum, a poly-
rhythm strummed
in air. This paper bird
pasted to a thin wooden
cross flies in the sky
like a fragile Icarus,
kept in air only by the thinnest

skein of desire.
I'd like to get away from earth,
soar to the sun, hide
in the spaces between
stars, but always
with some thread
to find my way home
to the labyrinth.

3

The cirrus blooms once,
one night only its opaline
fragrance gossamers the saguaro,
prickly pear, and manzanita, then
withdraws into a dark tuber to await
another blossoming in another year.

But every morning, every
afternoon, dark finger-
tipped wings circle
the desert sky, their narrowing gyres
the vortex of death. In dreams
I swirl down toward darkness as
a pearl-like flower rises higher
and higher above me.

4

The day I cut the locusts
on Huckleberry Island,
my chain saw spitting
thick sappy sawdust into
the heavy air, one tree,
bound and tethered by ivy,
wouldn't fall.

I guyed it with ropes and
cut it in sections
then noticed I had cut
a bird's nest in half,
the fledgling jay clinging
to the severed cup.

That night I dreamed the bird,
terror of staccato saw and
our black cat climbing.
The next morning I ran
to see the nest.

5

I flew to Christ in fits
and starts, yet he caught,
held me in the tight
fist of his grace.
When I fled from his nails
he opened his palm
to let me fly. Kited
by his fierce love, I soared
toward the surgical sun
then swooned into the nest
of his cupped right hand.
His crown was beryl and
bloodstone. His left arm
raised to the square.

Fishers

(fishing with my son on the Upper Weber)

In the last days of summer
we walk through tall grass
to the river long before
the sun spills over the mountains.
As we cast into morning air.
he flits like a water skeeter,
impatient for the taut nudge,
the sudden pull. "Be still,"
I say, "You'll scare the fish."

the river rolls over rocks
tumbling mauve and ochre stones

Still he stalks the fish,
an ancient angler
crouching in wet grass.
"Where are all the fish?" he asks.
"Here, where the current slides away;
There, by that big rock."

there, where the shards of morning
break deep on stippled stones
where clouds wash over watery weeds

Shadows recede against the mountains.
He asks, "Where do fish come from?"
"Some have been here a long time;
others are planted each year."

they swim from secret pools in the sky,
from starry rivers among the spheres, like birds
that fly through seas on fluent wings

"Have there always been fish?"
"As long as anyone remembers,
long before your grandfather and
your great-grandfather, long
before the Indians were here"

ancient fish swim down the headwaters of time
from old lakes deep as skies, where Indians wait
for rain on a seamless shore

Still the fish ignore our hooks
and still he wonders,
"What do fish bite?
What do they like to eat?"
"Sometimes corn and salmon eggs;
night crawlers are usually best,
although they love insects."

insects with iridescent wings
swim in the wind—mayflies and moths,
bumblebees and beeflies, golden-eyed lacewings
and black-winged damselflies dance before
shifting and sliding rainbows

"What kinds of fish are there?"
"Mostly trout here—rainbows,
a few browns. Over in the lake,
perch and bluegill."

sturgeon old as stone,
walleyed pike and yellow perch,
black bass, mackerel, and blue pickerel,
brown trout, rainbow trout, and silver salmon
glide and turn in the crystal light
their scales catching slanted sun

"Did you go fishing with granddad?"
"When I was a boy, we'd get up
at three in the morning
and drive over Mount Hood
to the Deschutes River where we'd
catch trout as big as your arm."
"Who's best, you or granddad?"
"Your granddad's pretty good.
He can catch fish where no one can."

In morning mist deer run before us
as in a dream; at the river my father watches
the wind and the water for signs I cannot
discern. Suddenly, a giant trout leaps into the air
to greet us, his mottled body silvers the sun
before my startled eyes

"But the greatest fisher of all
lived a long time ago. They called him
the Fisher King, and the fish of all
the waters listened for his voice, and
when he called them or when he sang
they came right him."
He arches his eyebrow, "Really? That's
just a story, isn't it Dad?"
"Maybe. Maybe not."

fish leap before him as he walks
on the waves and whales praise him
from the great green sea; he casts
his net into the brine and heaves it
brimming into the boat, and at
the psalming of his voice
the fish dance about his feet

"Dad! I've got a bite!"
His pole arches against the sun
and dips into the river.
"Hold him! Reel in, reel in!
That's it, don't lose him! Steady now."
The stippled trout flops
at his feet; he watches it with wonder.

When the sun reaches its zenith
my son and I turn from the river and
walk toward the mountain
through summer air filled
with incense of sage.

RELIGIOUS

Breath

At Treasures from Sinai,
an eleventh-century icon:
angels and shepherds surround
the Christchild.

As a small boy stares intently,
I say, "See—the donkey is looking at Jesus."
His father, an Orthodox priest
in a black cassock, says,
"When Jesus was born
all creation gave him gifts:
heaven gave him stars,
the earth gave him straw,
and all the animals gave him breath."

Lying in the manger, Jesus feels
the moist breath, warm
as the light on his face, breathes
wheat and barley,
redolence he will remember
when he multiplies loaves
and when the Devil tempts
stones to bread.

On the many nights when he has no place,
he lies down with the animals, escaping
into sleep on new-cut hay.

Riding into Jerusalem
over carpets of straw and flowers,
palms and tree branches,
hosannas ringing, he remembers
the friendship of beasts, and, for the first time
sees the black furred cross on the donkey's back.

Somewhere Near Palmyra

"The glory of the City was the temple of the sun."
—*Will Durant*

He saw something that morning
deep among the leaves
burning against the Eastern sky—
the sun and suns,
radiance enfolded
in oak and elm,
visages of light
luminous as seer stones
rinsing the still grasses,
personages of fire,
jasper and carnelian
dispersing the morning dew:
images that bore him
through dark of night,
terror of loneliness,
blood of betrayal,
the ache of small graves,
to death from the prison window
where, wings collapsing
through the summer air,
he fell—

And I know, kneeling
among the secret trees
this winter morning
where no birdsong rings
among the barren bush
and no leaves spring green,
where darkness thickens and gathers
among the withered weeds
and my tongue is a fish
under the river's roof,
that I too see what he saw—

sun, light, fire—
images of glory
flashing through the
morning mist.

Sabbath Baptism

In 1886, Sister Sallie Stephensen
of Fairview, Idaho, was possessed
of an evil spirit for a sabbath of weeks.
The congregation fasted and prayed, but
the spirit persisted, and so the elders
were called, eleven in all.
Pouring a goodly portion of consecrated oil
on her head from a small blue vial
that had crossed the ocean,
plains and mountains,
they commanded the spirit out—
but still it wouldn't come, so
after consulting the bishop,
they baptized her once a day
for seven days.

At the Sabbath meeting eleven elders stood
as witness to the power of the priesthood,
after which Sallie testified
that the spirit was still in her.
The benediction over,
they took her to the river
and baptized her seven times again,
it taking four of them to put her struggling
body under, the remaining seven
bearing witness that no hem of her
blue muslin dress nor tress of her long red hair
remained unimmersed.

When she arose for the seventh time,
gasping, water spewing from her mouth, she exclaimed,
whether from exhaustion or relief,
"Enough! It has gone from me."

She lived to be ninety-two and was present
at the baptism of all her children, grandchildren,
and great-grandchildren, but never again
rose in testimony meeting.

Baptism

The old man is lowered into the water.
At the moment of burial
he remembers his mother,
thinks of the time before time when,
laboring him out of her saline,
she held him new against the world.

Rills steaming from his gray head and beard,
he embraces the baptist, holding him
as fiercely as he held his mother
that first hour. All darkness between
remains buried in the font
and will flow to the great ocean where
salt again washes all things new.

At St. Bartholomew the Great

"Fear not, little flock, the kingdom is yours
until I come. Behold, I come quickly."
(Doctrine & Covenants 35:27)

Leaving Wren's great church, where
multitudes stream and swell and
God is defined in splendor and space,
I walk down King Edward and Little
Britain Streets to the old Norman church
where a few congregants pray
on worn stones.

This morning we kneel to face
one another across the choir.
At the crossing, our psalms and praises
rise to fill the rounded arches
in a curve of love.

When Christ comes again
some bright morning,
he will fly up the Thames, passing
St . Paul's baroque and Byzantine dome to
the sanctuary at St. Bartholomew's
where shopkeepers and clerks
will bow before his kingdom come.

At St. Paul's Cathedral

(The annual service of the Most Distinguished
Order of St. Michael and St. George)

The choir enters followed
by the College of Minor Canons,
prebendaries and the Bishop of London.
Next, the Companion of the Order,
Knights Commanders,
Squires carrying Banners,
the Gentleman Usher
of the Blue Rod,
the Chancellor
(preceded by a Squire carrying his banner),
the Prelate
(preceded by his Chaplain),
the Lord Mayor Tenens,
bearing the Pearl Sword,
H.R.H. the Duke of Kent
(Grand Master of the Order)
H.M. the Queen
(Sovereign of the Order),
H.R.H. the Duchess of Kent, and finally
the Queen's Bodyguard of
the Yeomen of the Guard.

As the procession moves down the nave,
the choir, on reaching Wren's great dome, sings,
All Creatures of Our God and King.
After the Lesson from Philippians
(read by the Grand Master),
the choir once again,
Blessed are the Pure in Heart,
after which all kneel in prayer:
Lord have mercy upon us.
Christ have mercy upon us.
Lord have mercy upon us.

Across the street, a mother
dressed in blue nurses
her newborn child.

Beneath an ancient mulberry
chauffeurs stain the pavement
mauve and purple.

Birdsong

Never again would birds' song be the same,
And to do that to birds is why she came.
—Robert Frost

The First Singer sang
as he fashioned feathers
and hummed as he shaped
tiny throats and tongues—
of the Red-winged Blackbird,
Indigo Bunting,
Scarlet Tanager,
the Meadowlark singing,
ringing through the reeds,

so that when they flew from his hands
and swam in wind,
they blazoned to all the garden round their singing,
his songs.

And when He made hers from ready clay,
shaping the hollow
of her throat,
sounding her voice apart from the birds
and Adam,
He breathed into her the music
of stars and spheres
of suns and deep darkness—
the sounds of all creation—
so they would echo from her
and all her daughters,
a rapture of praise
ringing through the world.

Deutsches Requiem

Behold, my days are as a handbreadth before Thee.
—(Psalm39:5)

Driving home last evening,
in the rear-view mirror
the sky so aflame it seemed
as if God had touched
the sun
and set the world on fire,
while on the other horizon
a Super Moon
luminous as Christ.

I have had for a little time toil
and torment, and now have found great
consolation.

—a heaven of fire,
communion of sky.

Salamander

"Nutrisco et extinguo"
—Legend of Francis I of France

*"God's people are true salamanders
that live best in the fire of affliction."*
—Thomas Brooks (1670)

When Alvin come back from the hill
he was in a sweat and tremblin'.
He says he looked in a box and saw
a salamander alive in fire,
and the fire was in his eyes
like small summer suns and it
come out and went into mine,
burning like God's own glory
and I was afraid.

> *And I saw sylphs of flame
> archangels of the sun, who came to
> Cumorah, ministering to the night
> their salamandrine fires illuminating
> and purifying the darkness.*

This was out by the barn, and
I said, Alvin, show me the box,
'cause I saw it in a dream
full of gold; and so we run
all the way to the hill and
was all out of breath, and
when we got to the place
Alvin says, look Joseph,
it's right there, under that bush!
And I looked and saw the fire, and
then the bush was burning and the
trees was burning and the whole
mountain was on fire, the river
was on fire too, flames all over
the water, joining and
crossing one another, but
none of it was burned.

*And I saw them standing in the fiery
heat, like the furnace of noonday
white as lightning, and beside
them was another, like the heart of the
sun, blazing with holiness and light
and the fire didn't harm their hair
nor singe their sleeves.*

Then Alvin was taken sick with a bilious
colic and was burnin' with a fever and
said many strange things, some of them
wonderful. And then he held me by the
hand real strong and tight and said,
Joseph, get the plates, whatever you do,
get the plates, and I said, Alvin, don't go!
don't go! And then he was gone, his eyes
still ablaze till father put his hand
on them and closed the lids.

> *I saw him in the realms of glory*
> *his whole body white and luminous as*
> *the stones in the box. I saw Adam and*
> *Abraham, and Alvin was with them, and*
> *I saw the transcendent beauty of the gate*
> *through which they entered and it was like*
> *circling flames of fire and the blazing*
> *throne of God ascending into light.*

And then it was dark and I
didn't dream for a long time,
and I said, Mother, the plates . . . and
she jest looked at me and didn't say a
word, and I turned to father, but he
wouldn't talk neither, and when I
looked at him, he jest shook his head
and tears come in his eyes.

All summer we worked the fields, and
when fall come we brought in the harvest,
but always I was thinking of
what Alvin said about the plates. In the
night I couldn't sleep and when the
new moon come I begun dreamin' again, and
then one night an old spirit come to me
three times and says, Dig up the gold.

I woke in a sweat and it was still dark.
I got out of bed real careful so's not to
wake Hyrum. I put some of mother's cornbread
in my pocket and took father's shovel and
went up the hill to find the plates.
I heard a owl way off in the trees and
was scared to go on 'cause it might
mean bad luck for me, but the words
of the spirit kept hauntin' me so I went on.

When I found the bush that before was
burning, I put the shovel in and dug
till I struck the stone box, and when I
took off the lid, light come burstin' out
and I saw the white salamander and then it
was gone but the old spirit was there and
he touched me three times—once on the
eyes and once on the ears and once on the
lips, and his fingers was like fire.

And I saw that everything was on fire:
eyes and images seen by the eyes were
on fire; ears and sounds heard by the ears
were on fire; lips and tongues and voices that
came out of them were on fire, and the Word
itself was a fire within a fire—everything
burning, burning, consumed by fire
and born again.

When I reached down to pick up the
plates the spirit struck me three times again—
jest like before, and he said, Bring your
bother Alvin, and I said, How can I bring
him, his bones are buried in the ground?
He said again, Bring your brother Alvin, and
I said, Should I bring his remains? but
the spirit didn't answer me.

I saw a valley full of bones, dry and
white, and a wind from the north and from
the night blew on the bones and they
were cold, and a wind from the south
and from the sun blew on the bones
kindling the fire shut up in them, and the
fire became the word out of the mouth of the
prophet and it consumed all who heard it, but
the bones danced to life and rose like
flames into the air, burning and turning
like a great fire bird circling.

109

When I reached into the box and
touched the plates, a shock went through me
like a sword of fire, almost melting my
bones' marrow it was so hot, and I cried
in agony of soul, Why can I not take them?
and the spirit said, You have not kept the
commandments, you have given in to temptations.
Get up and see the signs in the heavens,
and learn from the mouth of God.

> *And I looked and saw the heavens like an*
> *endless sea of light—the sun, a glorious*
> *luminary of the skies, and also the moon*
> *rolling in majesty through the heavens, and*
> *also the stars shining in their courses. And*
> *then all around me darkness grew into trees*
> *whose black branches shut out the light*
> *and I was left alone in the very heart and*
> *soul of darkness, and the branches were*
> *burning all around me, and their flames*
> *black as night began to burn my flesh.*

And I cried aloud, O God, forgive me, I
am jest an ignorant and wicked boy. Why
did you let Alvin die? He was the most
righteous one. I don't know, I don't know
about the sun and the salamander. I can't
see, it is so dark and my mind is on fire!
And then I saw the fire turn to blood
and I was falling from a high window
and as I looked up the sun fell
into blackness and I cried, O Lord, my God!

And I heard a voice like pure flame
pierce the burning darkness and it said
I have chosen you in the furnace of affliction
I will destroy you with a consuming fire or
I will purify you with a refiner's fire,
your heart must choose.
If you will burn away
your sins, I will make my words in your mouth
fire that you may warn the nations,
I will make your words a flaming sword
that you may slay the black dragon,
the fire drake of darkness, and touch
the hoard of gold
that it will come alive in your hands
to call my people
to the endowment of light.

And I awoke and was cold and afraid.

Via Dolorosa

At San Juan Bautista
on a cold February morning
I walk the stations of the Cross as
hundreds of blackbirds
rest on reedstalks.

I

Against a cobalt sky Pilate
washes his porcelain-white
hands. His wife's dreams
frozen in darkness.

II

Black mud hens flutter across
the pond like skipped stones.
The first heft of the wooden beam
dents his shoulder with dull fire.

III

He stumbles under the weight
like an ox weary of the wine press.
The shadow of eucalyptus
darkens the water.

IV

Mary weeps.
Iron oxide stains the stone wall
and runs to ground.

V

Where Simon lifts the rough-
shaped tree, dark leaves
rot at the pond's edge.

VI

She wipes his brow
with linen the color
of papyrus and holds it to her face;
a red-winged blackbird
begins its song.

VII

He stumbles again
and the sky presses down
like an angry anvil.

VIII

The daughters of Jerusalem moan
in the congregations of grief
like a chorus of mourning doves.

IX

An ancient oak—dark gnarled
galls, black, brown blight.

X

Dice roll on his seamless robe—
black dots like serpents eyes.

———

XI

Poison oak entwines the myrtle;
a green snake among
purple blossoms.

XII

The surrogate mother
the new-found son
embrace beneath the cross.

XIII

The cry of the Ruby-crowned Kinglet
echoes the hills and the darkening sky.

XIV

No world.
No words.

The Cradle

Joseph planed the cedar plank angrily
as he thought of Mary's belly
swollen beneath her tunic,
her new shyness a gulf between them.

She wept against his accusations.
An angel? Glory enveloping her? Something
she couldn't name coursing through
her body like golden light?

Shavings mounding at his feet
like coiled snakes, he continued
shaping the wood.

She came to the shop, touched
his face. When he did not respond,
she turned back to the house. When
she was gone he listened to the wind
like the whispering of his plane on cedar.

The scent of the wood mingled
with the sweetness of her new-washed skin.

Staying Alive in Priesthood Meeting

I've heard this lesson many times—
where we came from, where we're going . . .
so I open my book:
Staying Alive: Real Poems for Unreal Times.

In the distance the teacher asks about death.
I turn to Glück ("There are souls that need/
death's presence") . . .

"My granddaughter . . ."—hardly audible from
Brother Arnold who never says anything.
I look up as he begins again, "Her iridescence . . ."
I'm startled by his words.
As the teacher resumes, I close
my book and imagine:

a rainbow, its refracted light changing
as the angle of vision changes, the
agglomeration of glory in such small
things as a piece of glass, a sea shell,
a child's soap bubble wafting heavenward.

Por Los Muertos

"I had not thought death had undone so many."
—*T. S. Eliot,* The Wasteland

At the Los Angeles Public Library
a Day of the Dead exhibit—
skeletons, skulls and bones alive—the dead
partying, dancing, drinking tequila, making love, going
about their lives underground, nothing much changed except
their skin is gone, and they are gone. In scene after scene,
the dead go on their deadly ways, unaware
that a few blocks away the other dead
slouch in doorways, sleep in alleys or walk
vacantly, their skeletons asleep
in their skins. Those dead are not playing
guitars, shaking castanets, or blowing trumpets;
no mariachis or corridos echo from their mouths,
nor do they frolic on Figueroa or dance down Olivera.
Unlike Los Muertos in the library, their skin is yellow,
their teeth brown, their hair matted, their eyes filled with blood.

In the library the dead are transformed. For them
everything seems a joke or a party. A skeletal mailman's leg
is being bitten by a skeleton dog,
and everyone laughs.

But all along Central—bloodshot eyes, smeared mascara, hanging flesh—
the dead go on dying, leaving Los Muertos hanging on the library walls
very much alive.

117

POEMS FOR RUTH

Ruth's Poem

You say I have never written a poem
for you, obviously forgetting those
I wrote before I knew how. Instead,
you say, I write poems for friends,
students, our children, myself, even
God, but not for you.

You recall poems about blackbirds,
St. Paul's Cathedral, the Great Buddha at Leshon,
persimmon trees in the Santa Cruz Mountains,
even a poem about love, but not that kind of love,
and not for you.

Where's my poem? You ask.
It's a fair complaint. After all, if I can
write poems about trees and cathedrals,
I should be able to write one for you.

I know only this: some day
when I'm walking along a street somewhere,
not even thinking about it or perhaps
thinking about being with you on that island
off Green Bay, a poem will come,
as poems sometimes do, and when it does,
it will be for you.

In the meantime, all the poems I have written,
even the ones you haven't seen,
are for you,
including this one.

Quartet/Duet

Reading poetry alone in our son's house
the day after Christmas,
light and shadow (from the old stone pine
in the front yard and the Scotch pine
in the corner of the room) fall
on these words from Eliot's Quartet:

> Love is most nearly itself
> When here and now cease to matter.

But, because you aren't here, now does matter
and love is truly, completely itself,
even though I am not.

Convergence

For half a century
our hearts—full
wounded
broken
in darkness
blessed
in light
have found
one
another.

A Message from You
on the Beach at Santa Barbara

I try to decipher
the calligraphy of seagrass,
punctuated by seashells
and small stones;
the imprint of birdwalk
and children's feet
barely visible through
the sea's salt erasure;
fragments of seaweed and sponge
and the imprint of tides:
wordless
inside
broken parentheses,
half a comma,
an apostrophe,
nearly an ampersand,
a starfish asterisk,
and at the end
a grave accent.

Citrus Paradisi

Even something as simple
as segmenting half
a grapefruit reminds me of you. I cut
around each small ruby triangle
as I did all those
mornings when we did this
together, flipping out
the white seeds then
with each spoonful savoring
the acid taste.
Now that you're not here,
I do this every morning
standing over the sink,
eating faster than I should,
remembering how
when you had finished
you always turned
the fruit on its side and slowly
squeezed out
the last drop.

Washing Your Hair in the Kitchen Sink

It is late morning and oblique autumn sifts
through redwoods on the white porcelain.
Stravinsky, out of season, on the radio
as we begin our morning rite. You bend
your head and I open the faucet spilling
warm water all over your hair.

Out the window the San Lorenzo wends
toward the Pacific.

I Could Say

The plum tree in our front yard
is a snowstorm,
　　　　although it has been said before;
the wysteria's cream and purple blossoms,
a diadem above the walkway,
　　　　although once said and again;
and my love for you is like the heart-shaped
morning glories climbing the stone wall,
　　　　as someone has said before.

I've said to you, even with you gone,
and say again,

it's spring.

Dancing

Alone,
in the kitchen this morning
I held out my arms
as when they were around you
when we danced
the first time in high school,
then in college,
at our wedding,
and the
pas de deux
over half a century.

The day you died,
we danced in the kitchen,
slow and awkward,
but lovely,
when I held you
the way I held you
this morning.

If I Choose to Remember

Blossoming trees in late spring
as if some profligate heaven
had mixed
majorelle and indigo
amethyst and azure—
this unreal blue,
a gift of jubilation for Persephone or you
as we came from the Temple that afternoon,
purple-blue bloom
everywhere.

And, if I choose to remember: Night-blooming Cereus
that flowers only one night in the year

to blossom our wedding bed (and soon),
its fragrance filling the room,

and orchids and jonquils, if I choose,
lilac and lavender, too;

day lilies and peonies,
hyacinths and gardenias,

sweet Sweet Alyssum,
baskets of extravagant roses:
false asylum

from loss of you.

I Will Carry Stones from the River
(Fernwood, Christmas Day, 2013)

No stone
marks the place
where we have chosen
to lie down together.
The sun shines as
in the fullness of summer
on this hillside where
I will soon place your ashes,
keeping some
to scatter
on the far hills
where I walk alone these days.

It is Christmas day and
only the sounds of birdsong
and the wind off the Pacific
come here.
We chose this place
so we could lie in full sun
and see the stars
at night.

The hill slopes upward to a grove
of oak and incense cedar
and downward to a vale
of eucalyptus,
but here it is all open.

Soon
I will carry stones from the river
to mark your place
then mine
when it is time to lie down
beside you:
two stones washed
into the San Lorenzo
from granite
outcroppings in the
Santa Cruz Mountains.

Over the years our children
will come
and then our grandchildren
and great-grandchildren,
and then in that
millennium of years
we too will come to see
these stones
and walk over the green hills
to the sea.

HAIKU

Ochre, magenta, bone
sonatas of moon and stone:
in the garden alone.

Eucalyptus leaves—
comma, parens, apostrophe—
punctuating spring.

Among cactus thorns
one bougainvillea blossom:
impaled butterfly.

A flock of red-winged blackbirds
rising from the green:
death in the Euphrates valley.

Off Twisselman Road
row on row of almond trees
only one in bloom.

.

These leonine hills
lounging in winter sun:
nothing stirs or roars.

Candles' holy fire,
anthems rising from the choir:
emblems of desire.

These taupe and mauve hills
punctuated by old oaks:
one hawk catches light.

Kyoto summer:
you away in the mountains,
my heart a snow field.

Poppies and lupus
along the coastal highway:
Camino Real.

Long glass hothouses
just off Esperanza Road:
undulating sea.

Memory's desire:
Georgia O'Keefe's "Red Canna,"
my body's fierce fire.

Winter log, huge stone,
grandsons one end, me the other:
found teeter-totter.

Two blue-gray herons
above the San Lorenzo:
ghosts of night-morning.

New maple seed pods
thrown from the bridge—
spring helicopters.

In the mountain pond
a first frog belches out winter:
dried reedstalks listen.

One salamander,
then three
and a black coiled snake.

Iridescent emerald wings
on my tea cup:
and it's still morning.

Selling sunglasses
outside the El Sol Hotel:
Nightime in Cusco.

Above these white walls
A single blackbird—then two:
no darkness, just joy!

Gravitational:
Following the right God home;
Our own bright star.

Machu Picchu Haiku

Hidden in mountains,
Incan citadel of sun:
My kingdom today.

In the Leningrad Metro
(after Pound)

These haloed faces candling night:
hallowed icons, arcs of light.

Freud

Took the lid
off the id.
When he was gone
we put it back on.

FOUND POEMS

Enacts the Work of Seeing*

In lines like these
every phrase
enacts the work of seeing,
and every new image
offers
new purchase.

*Sven Birkerts' review of Joseph Brodsky's Collected Poems in English, New York Times, 17 September 2000.

Catastrophe*

Nothing creates
confidence
like catastrophe.

After the mind breaks,
it stiffens;
in the aftermath of grief,
certainty.

In a time of war,
complexity
is suspected
of sapping.
A mental
curfew
is imposed.

*Leon Wieseltier, "The Catastrophist," New York Times Book Review, 27 April 2007).

Two Persimmons*

a. a medium-sized tree with
hard fine-grained wood,
oblong leaves and
greenish yellow or
greenish white
bell-shaped flowers
followed by a
pale orange to
reddish orange
several-seeded berry
that is edible when
      fully ripe
but usually
         extremely astringent
           when unripe.

b. a strong brown
         that is
redder and deeper
     than average russet and
redder and duller
     than rust.

*Webster's Third Dictionary, *1961.*

Missa Solemnis*

The Missa's fugues
spit out at great speeds
in twisted,
dense,
crossing lines—

a breathless,
teeth-grinding vigilance:
one slip,
and derailment
is upon you.

Even deaf composers
hear music
without middlemen:
no violins to scrape,
pianos to pound,
or high notes
to attack.

The universe is fashioned
not by fiat or force,
but by seducing
the elements of chaos.

*Bernard Holland, "When Composers Make It Hard, Fright and Strain Become
Muses," New York Times, 1 June 1999, B1,3.

Bibliography of Published Poems

"At St. Bartholomew the Great," *Wasatch Review* (1993).

"Baptism," *Dialogue* 38:2 (Summer 2005).

"Black Handkerchief," *Dialogue* 40:2 (Fall 2007).

"Breath," *Dialogue* 46:2 (Summer 2013).

"Easter," *Dialogue* 46:2 (Summer 2013).

"Echoes of the Han Shan Bell," *Lithuanian Association of North American Stu*dies, 1 (1996).

"Famine and Scarcity," *Dialogue* 47:4 (Winter 2014).

"Elegy," originally published as "The Creatures We Kill," *West/Word* 7 (Summer 1993).

"Fishers," *Dialogue,* 17:2 (Summer 1984), 96-99. Reprinted in *Harvest: Contemporary Mormon Poems*, ed., Eugene England and Dennis Clark (Salt Lake City: Signature Books, 1989).

"Forgotten Birds," *Dialogue* (Spring 2018).

"Gene at Wilder Beach," *Proving Contraries: A Collection of Writings in Honor of Eugene England*, ed., Robert A. Rees (Salt Lake City: Signature Books, 2005).

"Gilead," *Sunstone* 6:1 (January-February, 1981); reprinted in *Harvest.*

"In St. Paul's Cathedral," *BYU Studies* 22:1 (Spring 1982).

"Heart Mountain," *Dialogue* 37:3 (Fall 2004).

"Liu Shahe," *Sunstone,* 139 (November 2005); also in Kenneth Lincoln, *A Writer's China: Bridges East & West* (Santa Barbara: Capra Press, 1999).

"Melancholia," *Dialogue* 46:2 (Summer 2013).

"Sabbath Baptism," *Dialogue* 46:2 (Summer 2013).

"Salamander," *Sunstone* 13:4, Issue 172 (August 1989).

"Somewhere Near Palmyra," *Dialogue* 13:3 (Fall 1980); reprinted in *Harvest.*

"Spring Comes to the Ming Tombs," *Sunstone,* Issue 136 (March 2005); also in *A Writer's China.*

"Tai Chi in Xian,"*Sunstone* 22:2, Issue 114 (June 1999); also in *A Writer's China.*

"The Cedars of Lebanon," *Dialogue* 37:1 (Spring 2004).

"The Dancing Beggar of London," *BYU Studies* 23:4 (Spring 1984).

"Wedding Flower," *Dialogue* 40:2 (Fall 2007).

"Yellow Crane Tower," *A Writer's China.*

About the Author

ROBERT A. ("BOB") REES is Director of Mormon
Studies and Visiting Professor at Graduate Theological
Union in Berkeley. Previously he taught at UCLA, UC
Santa Cruz and UC Berkeley and was a Fulbright Pro-
fessor of American Studies in the Baltics. He is the edi-
tor or co-editor of *Proving Contraries: A Collection of Writ-
ings in Honor of Eugene England* (2005), *The Readers' Book
of Mormon* (2008), *Why I Stay: The Challenge of Discipleship
for Contemporary Mormons* (2011) and *Fifteen American
Writers Before 1900* (1971). He has just completed *Ameri-
can Dreams* a play about the American Renaissance. His
poetry has appeared in such publications as *Dialogue,
Sunstone, West Word, Onthebus, BYU Studies, Exponent
II,* and in various anthologies.

www.ingramcontent.com/pod-product-compliance
Lightning Source LLC
Chambersburg PA
CBHW051800040426

42446CB00007B/452